TERRITORY

TERRITORY

Andrew Forster

FlambardPress

First published in Great Britain in 2010 by Flambard Press
Holy Jesus Hospital, City Road, Newcastle upon Tyne NE1 2AS
www.flambardpress.co.uk

Typeset by BookType
Cover artwork © Hugh Bryden
Design by Gainford Design Associates
Printed in Great Britain by Cpod, Trowbridge, Wiltshire

A CIP catalogue record for this book is available from the British Library.

ISBN: 9781906601157

Flambard Press wishes to thank Arts Council England
for its financial support.

Flambard Press is a member of Inpress.

The paper used for this book is FSC accredited.

Contents

Acknowledgements

Thanks are due to the editors of the following magazines, where some of these poems, or earlier versions of them, first appeared: *Groundswell, Cencrastus, The Eildon Tree, Poetry Salzburg Review.*

My thanks also to a number of friends whose perceptive comments on this collection at various stages have helped shape it: Michael Symmons Roberts, Vicki Feaver, Polly Atkin and Josephine Dickinson. Finally, thanks once again to Amanda Hunter for sharing the journey with me.

An earlier version of this collection was submitted for the MA in Creative Writing at Manchester Metropolitan University and won the Michael Schmidt Prize for the outstanding creative portfolio.

The Leadhills Road

Cars and lorries bound for Carlisle and Glasgow
are baffled by a straggle of alder and bird-cherry,
but this road, running alongside, abandons them
behind the scrubby depths of the Lowthers,

dipping and climbing, struggling for breath.
On either side paths dangle like loose threads,
leading to drystone pens, flickering streams
and a single house fencing in the open land.

Suddenly the ground on the right falls away
into a lead-gutted valley, rocks trickling like tears.
On the left it slopes up, darkly-planted
with spruce, silently shedding needles on soil

while the road tilts, a frayed tightrope.
Veils of cloud drift, ghosting the landscape
but around a bend, surprising as a light
at the end of a tunnel, the village rises.

The road widens, collapses into ruts
but picks itself up, squeezes past
clusters of tired cottages, the wind sighing
through cracks in the rendering.

Territory

With half a dozen bitumened posts,
hammer, spade, measuring wheel, calculator
and an Ordnance Survey map
with an L-shape scratched in scarlet pencil
by a solicitor, we are marking out
a piece of this hill that belongs to us.

The story is the land was parcelled up
when the leadmines closed, random shapes
given in compensation, but stories
are passed around the village like charms.

In the rising wind you scale up the map
and I pace it out. At a corner I try to dig
a hole for the pencil-sharp posts
but something in the grass refuses to give:

a rusted length of barbed wire, a fence,
collapsed by time, the former owner
letting the land go to wilderness.

With a pull the wire slices the grass
but I'd need a stronger tool to cut it free
so push it carefully to one side,
spade out a heap of stony soil.
You hold the post in place, I hammer it,
the blow hitting the hills and bouncing back.

In Search of the Sea

High on the broken spine of Great Lowther
I thought I'd see the coastline in the distance;
but here, where chance has dropped me,
there are only slopes of brittle heather,
and hills beyond almost identical hills,
gnarled and threadbare as old labradors.
The rush of wind is a pointless argument
and even the rabbits take their time,
ignore my heavy-booted stumbles.

I want to walk that old familiar path
where the salt breeze carries musky scents,
through grass too heavy to hold its own weight,
to a shard of beach awash with kelp, wrack
and coloured bottles labelled in cyrillic.
I want to brave the screams of gulls,
watch sunlight turn the sea to chrome
and listen to the long satisfied breath
of waves stretching out on sand.

Back home I paint walls aqua,
place pottery fish on shelves
and pieces of driftwood in corners.
I line the bathroom with shells,
hang photographs of rockpools
beside the stairs and, by the window,
a painting of a harbour with fishing boats
busy with crew, eager to hoist anchor
at the turning of the tide.

Shafts

They're all over Broad Law, these small enclosures:
rough wooden stakes, spaced and strung together
with barbed wire, bare of any explanation
but solidly there, like a Stone Circle.

The surveyor said *The hills have more holes
than a Swiss cheese.* On an old map I count
fifty-three mines in a five-mile radius
underpinning the streets and houses.

Their names are a litany of frankness
and wishful thinking: *George's Coast,
Labour in Vain, Weep No More,* names
that vanished from the hill with the flowers.

Behind the wire nothing distinguishes
the dried grass from the rest of the slope,
except a slight depression in the straggle
of yellow: the opening of a shaft

or a trick of the light. As the late sun
grips the hilltop with tired red fingers
the fences are rings of strange celebrants
linking hands, refusing to disappear.

Galena

We walk up Hunt Law, Peter and I.
My gaze is fixed on the late sun ahead.
I want to shrug off the weight of the day
to the rhythm of boots on the rock-strewn path.
Peter stops to prise a rock from earth.
Underneath, tiny spires of crystal glint,
an architect's dream of a city.
I hunker beside him. A moment ago
this was a rough, uneven track, but now
crimsons, pinks and jades sparkle in the dirt,
tiny jewels scattered on the arid hill.

He traces a vein of rust in a stone.
'Iron,' he says, 'but *this* is what it's all about.'
His arm sweeps the village below:
a street of terraced cottages struggling
to catch its breath, a few rows of patched houses
hanging on for dear life. 'Galena. Lead.'
His thumb smudges a band of black, shining
in the last light, so small you could easily miss it.

Rain in Leadhills

Ghosts dance in the village today,
their silhouettes slight darkenings
in the gusting rain, like traces
of a rubbed-out pencil sketch
still visible beneath a new drawing.

The miners that named this village
are free of hewing ore in tunnels,
trying to find space to swing a pick,
envying galena that is carted
into daylight and rinsed in the burn.

Now they wring each moment from the air:
stretch to full height, bend their knees,
clap hands like pine branches cracking,
stamp feet like a slate smashing from a roof,
sing in the deep bass of the wind in the street
and throw fistfuls of rain at windows
of cottages too small to contain them.

You Call This Rain . . .

. . . then you have never stared from a window
at a sky stillborn, churning with darkness
that can't imagine a glint of light;
looked at rose petals spattered on the lawn
edges brown and wrinkling like paper.

You haven't seen grey stone dampened to black,
watched water slosh from gutters and spew
from downpipes, course down the street
gathering old cans, wrappers and sticks,
shunting them in a rattling, hopeless surf.

You have never heard the relentless drip
into a bucket dumped beneath a ceiling
where water has run like a mouse beneath
the slates to find the tiniest opening,
staining the board, softening it to pulp.

You have never watched a river
lift its level until the Weir is a memory
beneath a foaming rush, and water bubbles
and slips over the lip of the stone wall
as quickly and quietly as a shadow.

This is a mere shortlived cloudburst
breaking the tension in the air,
sparkling in the sun like a glimpse of hope.
We should welcome it with arms extended,
drink it in like a tree's yearning roots.

But I have squelched through pools on gentle lanes,
my shirt soaked almost transparent, heavy
as if drowning, and I have listened
to the weak retch of a car, trying to coax
a spark from plugs which have given up the ghost.

Dorothy Wordsworth in Leadhills

Only falcons should live here. In thin air
she stares over the yellowing slopes.
Their mule stumbles on the stony track.
William pulls it into line. She and Coleridge
are thrown together in the rattling wagon.
The village appears and vanishes
with the bends in the track, like a mirage
in this high grassy desert. Stone cottages
squat: alone, clustered, or in vague rows
as if rolled like dice from the hills.

Coal-carts screech, miners' shouts crowd the street
unruly as the tuning of an orchestra
with no conductor to call them to order.
Here and there, beeches break out of knolls
spreading canopies of leaves, and by each house
kail-garths and potato beds are laid out
like altars, rich green against dry earth,
a reward for their humble worship.

Determined to record everything
she shouts at William to stop as a miner
limps from what she thinks is a school
holding a leather-bound book. Voice frayed
and skin like parchment, he unfolds
a letter of library membership
and shows her the copy of Shakespeare.
'We have plenty of time for reading,'
he says, pale eyes distant as the sea.

Later, needing to find her own bearings
she climbs to the burial ground and sits
on a rise, in the shadow of the giant bell
which tolls in emergencies, journal open,
gazing at untidy rows of weathered stones
drowning in the unkempt grass.

Wanlockhead

1. The Village

Rows of cottages, spread into the valley
like the fingers of a broken hand.
The road through the hills skirts across the top,
the village lying down in its blind field.
It seems stopped, this place, as still as
the narrow-gauge railway halted at its border
unable to bring Sunday passengers further,
the track running out in its grassy trench;
or the empty asphalt with its plastic sign
advertising petrol. Sheep swagger
on the trails between buildings. It's hard to see
where the village ends and the museum begins,
public cottages found among the private
like seams of ore running through rock.

2. The Miners' Cottage

Each room laid out as in different times,
rough wooden cots replaced by polished beds
as we move to the age when windows weren't taxed
guided by a trail of stories:
of the mine owners who paid wages
then took them back for food and tools,
of the village caring for widows and orphans,
and of Jenny Miller, crossing the hills
to her sister's wedding, who lost her life
in a sudden blizzard, but who is seen
sometimes, when the sun drops behind Great Lowther,
skipping through the tangled grasses,
swinging her wicker basket of flowers,
living entirely in the moment.

3. The Mine

A deep scar in the face of the hill.
There's no concession to comfort.
Apart from the rope of bulbs strung across
rock walls, it is as it must have been:
the tunnel almost too narrow to turn in,
air chill with the reek of rock-dust and lead,
a steady drip of unseen water
itching at the mind like an open cut.
More stories: of children washing ore
in the burn in which they would wash themselves,
the voice of the guide like a line paid out
to help us find our way in, then back
as the tunnel runs on, deeper
into the hillside, far beneath the village.

4. The Miners' Library

On top of a low hill, its white walls shine,
attracting light that reaches no further down.
This is where the miners came when they left
the darkness for the day. Windows spill light
onto oak floors and shelves of volumes
conserved in crimson leather: Scott and Burns,
of course, Wordsworth, Coleridge, but others too,
titles stamped in gilt, matter of fact:
Travels in Constantinople, Eastern Religion,
access prevented by a rope barrier.
There's a wax model of a stern librarian
and a recorded voice spelling out rules:
each book may be borrowed for one week,
the cost of damage must be reimbursed.

Retreat

Once a month they escape the world of tube-trains,
deadlines, traffic jams, to slip on *country selves*
with their woollen shirts and cement-spattered trousers,

slowing their pace in the time it takes
to break an orange crate into kindling
and fire the stove enough to boil a kettle.

It's their *stone tent*, a one-room cottage in the hills,
one step from derelict: gravel levelling
the earthen floor; walls stripped of lath and plaster;

toilet and sink gleaming white in the corner;
a light-fitting rigged to the single socket, hooked
to a ceiling beam dry as an old biscuit.

Each time they advance the house a little bit further,
sanding a casement, stripping the door, screwing
a bracket for a hanging basket to the outside wall.

As the weekend progresses they move in and out
of the path of the phone-mast, mobiles bleeping
to reassure them when they're back in range.

Painting the Summerhouse

It's late in the year for this, but the rain
hasn't paused and weeks have run together
like watercolours on wet paper.
The clean wood of the summerhouse shines
against the lank green of the hillside,
but even in December clouds can vanish.
This keen light brings the hills close enough
to touch: green shades dark against the blue sky.
I steady the ladder in the soft soil, cold
biting my hands as I climb to the apex.

Sounds drift towards me like woodsmoke:
a radio playing *Desert Island Discs*;
the toll of the church's single bell
sounding slightly warped and out of kilter;
a dog barking like the repeated cough
of an engine refusing to fire;
something like a distant swarm of bees
which could be someone taking a chainsaw
to a storm-felled tree; and the sharp crack
of someone else splitting logs with an axe.

I add my sounds to the Sunday morning:
the ladder's metal scrape as I climb;
the chime of the tin lid placed on the roof;
brushing the green stain into the wood
with the soft shuffle of a jazz drummer,
to make it a part of the landscape,
protecting it from winter's damp grasp.
A woman I don't know waves from the road.
I work with the grain, my breath steady,
hanging white and still in the crisp air.

Lamb

It's a tiny perfection of fleecy white,
circling next door's lawn like a puppet,
its bleats high and rapid as an alarm.
It must have leapt the sloping fence
at the one point where its low enough,
then couldn't find its way out again.

A ewe bolts through the grass to answer
the lamb's cries with her own. I walk over
to lend a hand: step over the fence,
chase the lamb to where it can jump to safety,
but the ewe lowers her horns to me.
She paces the fence but not far enough
so ewe and lamb can only mirror each other,
calling from either side of the wire mesh.

Rabbits

Not the soft, white, pink-eyed surprises
magicians draw from mysterious hats;
or the black-and-white English I kept as a child
and had to be reminded to feed and clean,
only occasionally releasing it
to nervously graze on the hankie of lawn.

These rabbits are self-confident,
unafraid to let their dusty-brown fur
stand against pale, windswept winter grass.

I grin, seeing something of the wild
lope into our dailyness, but you see
all your plans for a garden
chewed up before your eyes,
a warren undermining the pillars
of the summerhouse we use as an office.

Instead of a simple wire fence, you talk
of tightly-spaced planks and narrow mesh
(entrenched in earth to prevent burrowing)
and of a barrier of lavender
to scent the border and send them packing.

Gnawing your lip, you wonder out loud
about phoning our friend with the rifle.
I look for traces of your ironic smile.
A rabbit springs forward, comes to rest
before another clump of grass, munching
with all the time in the world.

Planting Trees

We follow the fence-line uphill:
lever out turf, dig two spades deep
making space to spread the misty roots.
We've been told it's pointless: too high,
windy, wet, the soil clogged with rocks.
If winter's icy fingers don't choke them
then rabbits will nip them in the bud.

But there's a will to bring trees back
to hills of yellow grass and heather
where only grouse are cultivated:
spruce, fast-growing, so spindly limbs
can lock into a windbreak; oak,
for the hollows; and flowering cherries,
pink and white against dried-out slopes.

I wall them in with sticks and netting.
None stand more than eighteen inches.
Looking back from the house, they are twigs
poking out of fragile fortifications,
the labels we tied to branches
with scribbled species and date of planting
flapping in the breeze like prayers.

Sheep

It must have been tempted by grass
longer and greener than the open hillside
and followed its nose into this space
between two fences, with no room to turn,
trapping itself between wood and wire mesh.

The others, drawn to follow the one
moving apart from the flock, padded after,
legs struggling under the weight of fleece,
each captured by inability to retreat
or refusal to accept the path is blocked.

By the time we arrive, they are wedged in,
heaped like so much jumble, faces
like masks. Quietened by fear, they tremble
against the sides of their accidental cage.
Cursing, the farmer lifts them like grain-sacks.

They sprint up the hill, then slow down
as if the memory of their ordeal
is already fading. They don't notice
the first sheep, stomach bloated, crushed
against the corner-post of our territory.

The Woman in the Woods

She's made her home on the line between worlds.
On her way back from the press of meetings
she steps from the rush-hour, Saint Francis
in a suit, and the blood-stained badger
trembling on the verge, quietens at her approach.

To the sett at the edge of the woods
she is den mother: their greying muzzles
tapping the glass of her porch at dusk,
they lean back on haunches like labradors
to catch the nuts she scatters in a rustling arc.

Once, when one lagged behind the rest,
its padding gait unsteady on the grass,
she cobbled a bed from a cardboard box,
draped it in blankets before the fire
and bottle-fed the badger back to health.

Yesterday, her door swung open at my knock
and through the windows at the back
I thought I caught a glimpse of her
rooting in earth in the shadowy dark
beneath the branches of beech and elder.

Panning

Shallows ripple around his waders
as he crouches, staring through the clear current
at mosaics of stones and silt on the streambed,
taking care to keep his movements tiny,
to minimise the disruption of his presence.

He's his own monument
at the bottom of these rusted slopes,
a celebration of quiet concentration
as still and absorbed in his task
as the heron that patrols this Mennock Pass.

He scoops the streambed with his pan,
thumbs calloused around the plastic;
keeps it moving, shaking and swirling
loose fronds of clay over the lip
to settle down through the water.

Ten years he's navigated these streams,
in the quiet spaces when tourists don't come.
He promised her a ring, crafted from gold
formed in these hills, whose patterns of light
and shadow have shaped their years together.

The sun kneads his neck. He shifts slightly,
smears sweat from his forehead, leans forward,
pores over the black sediment
and sees an unmistakeable glint
in the ragged mess of iron and lead.

Into the Hills

After scanning the map
and dialling the weather forecast
I don my waterproofed jacket,
serious boots and woollen hat.

The path winds through the long grass.
The street weighs me down
with its passing cars and everyday noise.
The path is steep and then
it levels and plummets
into a tremendous valley
and climbs again.

The hills are another world.
Here, buzzards swoop
across the valley floor
and the impassive face of rock,
stoats run through heather
and a single blue poppy flowers.

The wind washes my face,
layers of hills sliding away
towards the horizon
and I see

the miner with stooped shoulders,
dust in the lines of his face
and eyes more accustomed to dark
who wants to feel his limbs stretch
and breathe the sweet damp air
in the few free hours he has;

and the gamekeeper
patrolling the land of his masters
but walking in his own footsteps,
watching for signs of fox
threatening grouse.

Here I find my own rhythm
in a landscape with a host of stories
in which I hope to play my part.

Pheasants

I steer around them. Too many
to be an accident: messes of russet feathers
gummed to the tarmac with blood

as though a car or truck had mown
into a cluster of them. Perhaps
there were several drivers, keeping score,

swerving to pick off stragglers
who flitted desperately, trying
to get back to where they came from.

Around a bend the road is clear
until I'm halted by a policeman's hand
warning me of the huntsmen,

dismounted, milling in the quiet road.
One, in red tunic, wielding a horn,
whispers to the officer who waves me on.

Beyond, horses roped to gateposts
stamp and whinny, while a line
of tweed-jacketed men on the verge

laugh and jostle each other,
their urine arching into the grass,
glittering briefly in the weak light.

Horse

She holds the reins and the horse waits, as if sculpted
from ebony, for judges with clipboards and pens.
It's her model of a horse, flanks rubbed down
and gleaming like a Rolls Royce. She's brushed the mane
until it shines, threaded it into tight plaits.
The tail is so clean she could use it to dust
her uniform of jacket, breeches, knee-length boots.

Does the horse want to win? Does it look past
another caress of the brush, or lump of sugar?
It doesn't strain the reins, just stands in line.
Only once its back-right hoof gently rucks the grass
and it raises its head, slightly, as if to steal
a glance at slopes beyond the tents and fences.

Mouse

It waits for the sound of our settling
to emerge from wherever it spends its days.
It's frantic scurry beneath the floorboards
or behind walls, drums into our dreams.
Some mornings a few chewed strips of paper
litter the kitchen, as if carelessly
dropped on return from a midnight forage
but that's all: no dark clusters of droppings,
no nest-like hoard of shreds and scraps.

It lives in a separate dimension
taking advantage of the spaces we leave.
We can shrug off this nocturnal squatter
as the small cost of countryside living,
not grudge a share of warmth in winter.
We don't wish to wake to the snap of a spine
but grey hollows hang beneath our eyes
while its echoes run around the house
as it scrapes and gnaws the joist beneath us.

Damselflies

They come in from the whispering rain
each time the door or window is opened:
dozens of them, sparks in the scratched dark,
riding the warm air into the kitchen.
Legs crackle with electricity, clumsy
as puppets. They closet themselves in corners,
clinging to plaster, or follow each other
in a linked chain like a pagan dance
around the hot glow of the lightbulb.

Is this their heaven? Perhaps they dream
of somewhere just like this, from their hatching
by the burn, throughout their month-long lives;
drawn here like salmon, against all odds,
by an innate, mysterious pull.
We leave them in peace. Later, empty shells
of them will litter the kitchen, brittle
and breaking at a touch, mere signs of something
that passed here, light and elusive as breath.

Encounter

It tumbles into the glare of my headlights:
legs a knot it is trying to untangle,
barrel-body too small for those legs,
face stubby and wrinkled as a crying child.

With barely time for me to stab the brake
it springs free of the headlight's snare,
carries itself through darkness like a weak flame,
vanishes beyond the huts of the old mine.

I search for a frame of reference.
Rumours of panthers roam the hills,
but up here only heather really offers shelter
and this was more the size of a calf.

Back home, 'Muntjack Deer' is your response.
I protest that we're too high, with no trees
but photos on the web are a perfect fit.
Sociable creatures, it must be lost.

I feel the faint ache of a mystery explained
and prefer to imagine a solitary creature
shambling over the hills, avoiding definition,
glimpsed by puzzled drivers finding their way home.

The Hare

For an instant my headlights catch it
as it crosses the mountain road: hind legs
propel it, muscle rippling through haunches,
front legs rushing to keep the rhythm,
ears pressed back like folded wings.

We can't grasp its nature from these glimpses.
Any attempt to hold it still and it stretches
its body, quivers like piano wire, twisting
free of any meaning we might impose.
It passes through our stories, a trickster

forcing us to shove down the brake
and take the bend with care, not jerk
the steering wheel and swerve, crashing
through the fragile barrier and hurtling
down the heather-smothered slopes.

I see it now at the side of the road,
tapping the tarmac with its clown's foot,
winter-white fur wrapping its neck,
body still brown, ears taut, testing the air,
searching for the next path to cross.

Pigeons on Motherwell Station

They defy logic, delicate pink claws
balancing plumped, leaning bodies
on a cable tacked to a frayed brick wall
behind the Westbound platform;
but as their heads turn slowly side to side
like spectators at a tennis match,
their trill is a chorus of contentment.

One steps off, almost casually:
an idle flutter of wings softens its descent
to the platform. Walking splay-legged,
somewhere between a waddle and a stroll,
it finds a path around the restless feet,
pausing to peck at something on the concrete
that the shoppers and commuters can't see.

Another flourishes wings like a phoenix,
ready to quit the station's constant dusk
and head for the fields, but its clattering flight
reaches only as far as the ledge
of the overhead tunnel that feeds the platforms.
It settles there, above the space between rails,
as if wondering which direction to take.

Hen Harriers

I could almost set my watch by them.
When the sun drops behind Hunt Law,
pulling light in its wake, the trio
tread air with blurring wings, up where
the steep slope of the garden flattens,
hanging over tangled grass like question marks.

Hen Harriers, marked by a white blaze
over their tails: the two males smooth grey,
the female's rich, shadowy brown
flickering in the uncertain light.

They grip the corners of an invisible net,
needle-sharp eyes piercing the grass,
until the larger male darts sideways,
drawing the others to hold the pattern.

The leader plummets like a stone,
springs back with a shrew in its claws
and climbs to the horizon, letting
the still-squirming load fall to its mate,
who clutches it at her breast like a baby
and follows, the younger male in their slipstream.

It's over in a minute. Dusk raiders,
they don't want to linger this close to lights
and the murmur of houses settling to evening.

But one afternoon, behind the village
I see them in their element, soaring
over the heather-matted valley, turning,
gliding back, stretching their wings
to an undreamt-of span, with no aim
other than to bask in the warm current
and live in the moment.

The Peregrine and the Rooks

Sudden as a cloud blotting the sun
he swoops, tawny wings thrown back,
hooked bill glistening, claws so sharp
that only a glance makes me shiver.
He drops behind the drystone wall,
this brief sighting a gift of the wild
on my drive home through the slow dusk.

But then he flies back, and curves round,
down this quiet lane, wings sure and unhurried
as waves on a beach on a still afternoon,
late light igniting the gold of its primaries.
Seconds behind, two rooks shoot up,
taking up position on either side, sentries,
their black alarm scoring the sky.

The peregrine seems unconcerned, the beat
of his wings doesn't speed up or falter.
The rooks are all bluster. He will allow them
to escort him from their feeding grounds,
let word of their bravery be signalled back.
He desires solitude not the chatter of rooks.
He will keep his power to himself.

November Music

I trudge through a morning sapped of colour,
coat tight against a damp wind, sickly-sweet
with fertiliser from fields being nurtured
after harvest. The days curl up like leaves.
All I want is to be home: brightness, heat.
From an open window the baritone moan
of a saxophone eases into the street:
a hesitant sorrow. I should move on,
not be caught listening to private grief
but it grips me like I might an acorn.
While I linger the music gives some relief:
fumbling notes transformed to an amber balm.
Somehow the pain found the strength to heal
itself, climbing steadily up the scale.

Picking Sloes

We've left it late. The bushes look ransacked:
the best already taken, those left over-ripe,
burnished sacs unable to contain
the weight of seeds, bursting at a touch
like a jacket popping a button.

But at last in this ragged new landscape
we've found a place where sloes grow.
You shove aside thorny branches
willing the bushes to give us something
we can sweeten through a bitter winter.

Soaked brown leaves carpet the verge.
Only a brittle rind of light
traces hills against the heavy sky.
Yet deep in the dark, woody tangle
a scatter of berries hang like purple moons

almost black, yet to cloud over. We gather them
until staccato rain spatters the grass.
We'll take this tiny harvest home:
prick with a fork, add gin and sugar,
and leave for a month. It could be enough.

Settling

No warning, just a wet splash on my hand
as I squeeze the last box into the bin.
Despite local legends of roof-high drifts
it's still a surprise, in November, when snow
spangles the afternoon like falling stars.

Back on the coast, once or twice a year
it filled the sky with glints of possibility
but with the salt in the air it didn't settle,
dissolving wetly on pavements and ledges
or under the rushing wheels of cars.

Here, it smoothes imperfections on scrubby ground.
In cottages on the hills, woodsmoke plumes
from chimneys and lights go on in rooms,
while the snow forms a new white page
waiting for me to make my mark.

Snow on New Year's Eve

The year creased its brow
quickly as a curtain falling.
A sudden swirl of snow
blurred the view from the window,
pulled a shroud over the streets.

The houselights shuddered
like a wire in a high wind
and then went out.
We coaxed a fire into light
with twists of last year's news.

It glowed red, certain,
casting a new light on you
reading out loud a story
by Edith Wharton
about a man in a storm.

Midnight's bells must have been
drowned by wind, or muffled
by snow, and when we climbed
the stairs we sensed
something important had been lost.

New Year's Morning

The clarity of the morning
is a resurrection
after the purgatory
of last night's storm.

Through the window, the road
is a clean black ribbon
promising an exit
between sharp banks of snow

but taps sputter air
and lights refuse to obey
the command of the switch.
Outside shovels scrape

and laughter chimes like
rusty bells as neighbours
clear paths to their doors,
exchanging news like gifts.

Picking my way through drifts
on the pavement, I hear
the water pumps lost power
when a cable fell

and a fire in the next village
drained the tanks. Unable
to glean more I turn
to my own door, and dig

out a path, heavy at first
but borrowing rhythm
from the others. Our words
write themselves in air

and in this common labour
I slowly find something
I thought stolen when the snow
cancelled all celebrations.

I toss the snow in a heap,
soiled white and crumpled
as the discarded pages
of another year.

Light, on a February Morning

The light, this morning, is like a stoat
scurrying across the road,
white bristles shining at the tip of its tail
as it disappears into the grass.

It's like a snowy owl
in the high branches of an elm
swooping down through the damp air
in a sudden rustle of wings,
claws latching around a mouse
and hauling it back to its perch.

It's like a deer
racing across the field in a russet blur
reaching the safety of trees.

The light this morning is like a heron
still as alabaster at the side of the burn
spiking a trout
with the javelin of its beak.
Its wings spread
and it rises from the ground with a slow beat,
vanishing over the leaden hills.

The Remains of Snow

They are still here, the rags of snow:
webbing the hillside,

nudging the fence like old polystyrene,
lying like moth-eaten lace on the pavement,

speckled with dirt from passing cars.
When the sun catches at a certain angle

they glitter with secrets as if about to thaw
but crunch stubbornly underfoot.

It's nearly April, when evenings
stretch like a peregrine's wings

but the snow remains, itching
at the mind like a splinter in a finger.

Is it that it's still around, with its sense
of being shaken and abandoned

inside a plastic dome, watching
flakes gather around a quaint church

or that it will certainly melt, trickling
down the street with its cargo of silt?

Late Winter: Mennock Pass

The morning stretches, buttons its jacket.
I scrape a skin of frost from the car windscreen
like fingernails scratching a blackboard
against the quiet of curtained cottages.
The engine coughs exhaust fumes into the street.
I pull away. Frost has etched each blade
of grass on the verges like white fur
and gripped the litter of last year's leaves.

The sun crests Great Lowther like a rheumy eye
slowly clearing, cutting swathes of green
through the frosted grass like a blunt sickle.
I drop through the pass, past sheep
burrowing through heather, and though I only
catch it in the corner of my eye, I'd swear
the heather is already flowering,
hints of green and purple on the brittle stalks.

The Mennock Water, lined with broken rushes,
glitters like cut glass as it bubbles over stones.
Under pines, a few clusters of snowdrops droop,
fragile, as if they might disappear
any second, but as I leave the pass,
pull out onto the Dumfries road,
I have to pull down the visor as light
drenches the windscreen with liquid gold.

Winter: Leadhills

It's the dry heave of a car's engine
                              on a lead-black November morning.

It's a dusting of snow
                    that no footprints disturb.

It's walking through cloud
                            that softens lines
between a dog's bark
                    and silence,
between emptiness
                and a firmly-flagged path.

It's the swagger of sheep
                        through a broken fence
                                        to close-crop the grass.

It's the roar of a chainsaw
                        cutting a storm-felled poplar into logs.

It's the unexpected path
                    behind a heather-smothered ridge.

It's a gate, barred,
                by a *Beware of the Bull* sign.

It's a heron
          frowning in the stream
                            for the silver glint of fish.

It's a vague smell of sulphur
                        after the rain.

It's the slow coaxing of the stove
                              with paper and sticks.

It's night falling quick
                    as the click of a switch.

It's the slow beat of a snowy owl ahead of us
                                    leading us on.

Winter Trees

Sculpted by the wind off the Solway
they mark the boundary of land and sea,
dark silhouettes against the tumbling dusk,
frozen in classical postures:

one's an athlete, testing his endurance.
Striations on bark show the twist in the trunk,
branch swung back like he's holding a discus
at the furthest limits of a parabola;

then there's a warrior, forked at the base
like legs firmly planted, stubby branches –
power concentrated in his squat trunk
ready to defend himself against any threat;

and the prankster, caught in the middle
of a jig, balanced on one thin leg,
conjuring chaos with dancing arms,
wind and waves in thrall to his whim.

The stillness of these trees is difficult to hold.
Any moment they will explode into movement.
Bare twigs tremble at each shift in the air.
They are the earth stripped to its nerves.

Cairnsmore of Fleet

Wind argues its way through the rushes,
muffling the gagging of ravens
and sending clouds scudding across the weak sky.
Eagles once nested on these unforgiving outcrops;
slopes were purple with heather, fertile
with rodents, but now they're dry and threadbare.

The land's been over-grazed, heather
over-beaten, burnt once too often
in the name of regeneration,
as if tongues of fire could ever reason
with nature. Land managers still dabble:

they've shipped in long-haired Luing cattle,
hardy for these chill heights, to graze
and break up the surface like a petrified skin
so the owners can resow heather
as if the hills are merely a windowbox.

Down towards Craig Ronald, wild goats
eye us casually, as they have for centuries
even before the monks claimed ownership.
They chew moorgrass, amble down the valley,
don't give me a backwards glance.

Wigtown Harbour

It crouches behind the town as if ashamed:
a slopped-asphalt carpark,
life buoy on a bleached wood pole
and two long-faced fishermen, legs dangling
over the jetty, lines swaying faintly.
Water drags itself through a narrow channel
between banks of swollen mud.

People shaped this landscape: an Earl
who wanted to leave his mark
didn't like the way the river curved
so straightened it like a piece of rope;
the Merse where Belted Galloways graze
made by tidewalls, so the retreating sea
would leave behind this salty residue.

Where the sun glances, mud glistens
inviting me to grab handfuls,
plaster my face, smooth the age-lines
from my weary skin. Grebes hop,
their prints acting as evidence
of the mud's firmness, but I know
I'd sink, softly, in its treachery.

Suddenly, two Mute swans, as pure white
as possibility, bank low in the warm air
and water splits as the tide turns,
river flowing out, sea flooding in.
The swans throw their wings back
in glorious surrender, glide down
to the harbour, skating in the mud.

Rough Island

Knowing how long we have before the tide
bubbles in through mud, we cross borrowed land,
splashing through shrimp pools and stepping over
tiny reefs of mussels and barnacles
which huddle together for protection
from carrion crows that would smash them on rock.
The sun plays down unfettered, and the wind
carries traces of staleness and abandonment.

The strangeness of the journey makes arrival
so vivid. A short scramble over shingle
and there's bracken, rosebay and knapweed.
It's trying to be its own universe,
this island, a colony declaring
independence, but it's shaped by the sea.
The sea layers the beach with shells, wears
down sandstone, inching higher with every tide.

A Northern Argus flits across, throwing light
back from brown wings. It will live a whole life
within these few acres. In depressions
on the beach, neat clutches of eggs, left
by plovers dragging wings in feigned injury,
drawing away foxes who slink
from the mainland in darkness, or us,
daytrippers, delighted with earning this island.

The Adder

I almost step on it, coiled on the wrack
among plastic bottles, yet more litter
abandoned by the tide. It hisses and I jump,
startled, but keep watching it: eyes of jet,
head a delicate hammer hinging back.
It looks as surprised as I am, and I'm caught up
in the strange symmetry of its markings,
black and brown like damp-stained parchment.
I've heard there are more of them now,
shrugging their way through milder winters.

The sky is moody with cloud, distant rain
muddy streaks over the horizon.
The sea curves down from its meniscus
slopping over rocks, inching forward
to lap the roots of flowering gorse.
We stare at each other, the adder and I,
each carrying a code the other can't decipher.

The Magpie

The sharp tap at the window scratches
at my unsettled sleep in this strange bed.
Careful not to wake you, I cross the floor
in this borrowed cottage in the woods
where we've come to see what's still between us.

In the porcelain light, a magpie
occupies the narrow sill, claws scrabbling
like grappling hooks, keeping its balance
with an urgent flap of wings, long tail
working side to side like a rudder.

I hadn't imagined them as pets,
demanding food with this insistent rap.
It's a rogue bird, cajoling me
to open the window just enough
for a dawn raid on something sparkling

or perhaps attacking its reflection in glass.
Fixing me with a jet eye, it turns,
heading for trees with a strange dipping flight
as if it is riding water not air.
We both seem out of our element.

Searching for bearings in the deserted morning
I stare over oaks and maples to Ullswater
gathering its silver as the light grows.
With a sudden flutter the magpie returns
placing a coin on the ledge, deliberate as a gift.

Lanty's Tarn

We shouldn't have started out.
Sweat streamed down my back and legs
as we fought through ferns up the tight dirt track.

The sun blazed in the brittle sky,
Ullswater lay like sheet metal below,
air caught fire in our lungs.

Over the hill, slopes of cindery grass
offered no relief as we dragged ourselves
down the old drovers' path.

It was always going to disappoint:
this flat pool of water, holding darkness within,
leaking into rushes like an inkblot.

A curve of cracked and flaking stones
defined one end of the Tarn, for drovers to sit,
murmuring in a close-lipped dialect.

A chill brushed my arms. We'd reached
the cold heart of our journey. A cloud
of midges teased, as if their shape held meaning.

Dragonflies plundered the lake,
the only traces of their raids
ever-decreasing circles on the water's surface.

Glencoyne Wood

It feels like wilderness, this woodland.
Oak, sycamore and beech climb the hill,
looking permanent as mountains.
Branches reach over slopes like giant insects,
armoured with bark, trailing leaves silver with rain.

Last year, a storm-felled oak blocked the track.
The hacksawed pieces, pushed up the bank,
are still there, bright with moss, the long grass
beginning to enfold them, the landscape
pulling the butchered tree back into itself.

Another oak has been toppled,
pulling up an island of peat in its grid
of roots, thick and sinuous as human arms,
leaving a neat space already filling
with water and alive with dragonflies.

Here and there are signs of intervention,
small courtesies: a tiny wooden canal
channelling water away from the bank;
a scattering of young oaks, crisp brave leaves
blazing from private wooden enclosures.

Down towards Ullswater, where bracken
tussles with broom on the cusp of flowering,
a Scots pine glows pink in the late sun,
the division of its trunk like two lovers
joined beneath a canopy of green needles.

Roe Deer

It crosses the lane ahead of me,
the lowering sun ruffling its coat,
highlighting the grey in its shades of brown.
The sureness of footing and fixed gaze
possess the narrow strip of tarmac,
making me pause in my evening ramble.

It strolls into the trees and I carry on
but as I reach the spot where it had walked
I feel something like an invisible arm
draped around my shoulders, and turn.
In the charged air of the wooded slopes, tense
with trees coming into leaf, the deer is still.

Its stare measures the space between us.
White Moss straggles up above me
and despite the breath of distant cars below
I'm caught in a silent communion.

The movement ripples down from its neck
and the deer turns and springs away, hindlegs
churning a colourful wake of last year's leaves.

Did I imagine the gleam in its eye,
the slight gesture of its neck as it turned?
It was almost coy, an invitation
to forget the path leading me back
to where I'd started from, and follow,

and the soft percussion of its hooves
as it dances through the trees out of sight
is a language I can almost remember.

Church by a Field with Goats

The congregation gathers by the doors
of the Norman church, its certainties
set in stone and oak but almost delicate,
patiently waiting in this bowl of green hills.
Stained-glass windows depict bible scenes,
colourful but modest, not greedy with light.

In the churchyard, grass neat as a football pitch,
headstones are laid in a perfect grid, smooth,
engraved, each garnished with a quiet spray
of marigolds, daisies or primroses,
none trying to outreach the others.
Here, the dead are held close to the living.

In the field behind the drystone wall
a herd of goats, black and white, neatly cropped,
march in pairs towards an open gate
as if about to be rescued from a flood.
Each is a mirror image of its partner,
steady, head bowed to the will of the herd.

Above, the sky is a tumbling wash of blue.
The rain starts, fine as silk, hardly felt
but seen as tiny fragments of silver
in the long reach of the white sun.
The congregation enters the church,
sit in polished pews before the altar.

Gosford Wood

You could be the first to enter here.
Between oak, pine and sycamore
are cylinders of stillness
solid as the trees. Copper leaves
drift across the floor and
swallow the sound of each footfall.

A log, shrouded in lichen,
glowing in green light, collapses
into dust as your foot nudges it
as if it waited just for you
and has now served its purpose.

You find a gentle bank, lie
cushioned by grass, in dappled light.
Time passes like a leaf unfurls
or ivy creeps around a tree.

A blackbird drops a song at you
and you clutch it: a lifeline.

Haweswater Dam

After the neat grid of narrow lanes, cut
between hedged and freshly-furrowed fields,
it's a shock: this stone and concrete wall
shaping the lake, buttresses like arms,
staking its claim in the bowl of sudden mountains,
beating the harsh light back from its surface;
a walkway wide enough for two to dance across
pausing to survey the lake like monarchs.

In the rosy shade of maples, the vision
of the Manchester Corporation
is faded letters on a painted board.
The lake is tight as a drum, opaque
and milky as a blind eye. There's no sign
of Mardale Church Steeple, though I have heard
you can see it below when the light is right.
Even the dead were moved somewhere else.

Silence shouts: no murmur of lapping water
or otter through grass, no jay whistling.
An eagle circles, darkening to a blot
before the sun. High, across the lake
a figure picks its way along the Rigg,
stopping and starting. It could be human
but in the haze of heat and distance
it is difficult to say for certain.

Places

We planned to live there, in that harbour
village as tiered as a wedding cake:
to shrug off the working day by strolling
the frail coastal path until we reached
a wilderness of tidal pools. We'd return
to sit on the sea-wall, eat fish and chips,
and watch the sun like a blood orange
peel itself into the water as it sinks.

But now I wake in this vale, beneath
the steady slumber of Silver Howe,
the end of a chain of events as sudden
and unexpected as a summer shower.
I'm pushing the boundaries
of the familiar, making nightly walks
to Rydal, Easedale, Elterwater,
slowly mapping a new territory.

We leave them behind, all the places
we never lived, let them turn sepia
in our memories but we like to think
there are shadows of us flickering
on those trails. When the light is right
they might be glimpsed by those passing through,
in space rescued from their busy lives,
plotting their own geographies.

Grasmere, January

for Jane

Walking into the village at lunchtime
the news about you weighs me down
like a rucksack overstuffed with what
I need but would rather be free of.
The scan revealed a shadow on your brain,
a tumour grasping the part of you
that might remember sharing poems
in Mathers' Bar, or mixed thali
in the Taj Mahal, and words of kindness
written on the back of postcards of landscapes;
the part of you that sees with such clarity.

Here, now, in the sharp January light
I can almost touch the smooth brow
of Seat Sandal, Helm Crag's scowl
and Dunmail Raise, that narrow pass
where the road goes north to where you are.
You planned to come and see me here
but I can only see this copper bracken,
dusty winter grass, and the line of hills
keen against the perfect sky, and think
of you in your cramped room, and try
to see everything as clearly as this.

Levens Moss, Winter

It stretches out below the village:
the *Lords' Plain*, a land partitioned
by distant owners, divided by hedges
of yew forced into horizontal growth
and glinting like iron in the weak light.

The Causeway runs around the plain.
Once a raft of thatched logs, a safe route
for horse-drawn carts, now it's a tarmac road
and tractors clank through summer nights
in the space allowed by heavy rain.

Beneath verges, wild with brambles and rushes,
the Cut reinforces the boundaries,
framing each field, its sides recently renewed,
smooth and brown, the stream thick and still,
ice chiming softly where the sun can't reach.

The fields are scribbled with pale winter grass.
Cows have been moved to different pasture.
Pylons march across, catching the last sun,
their angles suggesting a turning away,
powerlines hanging low between them.

Cycling

You walk the gleaming green bicycle
from the garage stuffed with boxes
we recently unpacked and dismantled;
mount the seat, gripping the handlebars
like a horse's reins, and edge to the gate
with gentle shoves on the gravel.

Wary of trusting a skill you haven't used
in years, you let the wheels feel the slope
between squeezes of the brake, your feet
touching the road as fingers might reach
for a lucky coin or a rosary.

At the start of the Causeway, flat as card
between the grid of fields, you half-stand
and start to pedal, with a steady breath
of rubber on tarmac, swaying slightly
as you try to find your younger self,
to get comfortable with the feel of tyres

on this new road. You lean to the left
and for a moment it seems the bike
will slide out from beneath you, and you'll fall
into the winter tangle of rosebay,
bracken and hawthorn beside the road.

But somehow you find your balance
and speed up, shooting towards Whitbarrow.
The ring of the bell is tinny and small,
just a scratch on this wide sky, but
repeated, it signals joy in the moment,
shouting at the landscape that you have arrived.

The Cinema Organ

He played, rising through a trapdoor in the stage
like the Morlocks from their underground labyrinth:
green, orange and yellow plastic lit from within
like a spacecraft. Waiting for *The Jungle Book*
we were hypnotised by 'Bare Necessities':
an orchestra, with the locomotive rhythm
of drums, conjured from the glowing machine.

He played on, last of the line, sometimes just for me
escaping bickering parents in the thinning velvet
of the cinema seats. His black tuxedo shone
in the river-damp air as he waltzed the warm strains
of 'The Blue Danube' from the keyboard, bringing
the sparkle and glitter of a Viennese romance
to the smoky streets of this Northern town.

If we listened we could still hear him
behind the Bingo caller whistling *Legs Eleven*
and the rush and burble of coloured balls
projected onto the empty landscape of the screen;
seats and carpets ripped away for vinyl flooring
and formica tables, where old friends let silent music
remind them of fumbles in the old twin-seats.

Now, as we cross fresh tarmac towards
the steel and plastic of the retail park, we pause
trying to make out a melody in the grinding gears
of buses cranking to a stop, in the wind breathing
through newly-planted yew trees, in the rich notes
of the river lapping, shuffling over the tiny weir
with a sound that could be a snare drum.

Driving to Prestwick

To know when to brake and shift gear
at each bend and gradient, to see
each white cottage before it appears:
this stumbling road surprises me
with its familiarity. I suppose
I drove it most days for nearly five years.

The green domes of the Lowther Hills
are less dramatic than the Cumbrian Fells
where I'm living now; hedgerows more ragged,
drystone walls bound together by
a much looser contract. This landscape
won't make a fuss or mind its language.

Around a bend by the picnic tables
and I'm driving on new black tarmac:
the road has been rerouted, the pass
which would take me to my old home
out of reach up a steep bank.

That is as it should be. I've moved on,
I'm passing through. The land will continue
to be shaped, but my version of it
is in me now, part of the private map
I add to, a lens through which I see.